What Reviewers Want: Get Inside One Reviewer's Mind.

D. L. Graham

A Reviewer's Guide for Authors with Study Guide Worksheet

Copyright © by D. L. Graham

Published by Twisted Rose Publishing

Cover Design © angel Graham of angel Art Studio

All rights reserved. This book or any portion thereof may not be reproduced or used in any manner whatsoever without the express permission of the author or publisher except for the use of brief quotations in critical articles or reviews.

ISBN-13: 978-0615612812 (Twisted Rose Publishing)

ISBN-10: 0615612814

DEDICATION

Dedicated to the Romance Diva's for teaching me how to improve my craft, in all ways. I've been learning —see!

Dedicated to my husband, Rob Graham, for believing in me. Your unwavering faith that I could and should write this guide. Constantly listening to my questions about how it sounded, and your enormous help in the editing process. I love you, Sir.

CONTENTS

	Foreword	i
1	Book Covers	1
2	Editing	7
3	Critiques & Beta Readers	17
4	Characterization, Plots, and more	20
5	Finding a Reviewer for Your Book	25
6	The Reviewer's Review & How to Respond	33
7	Doing Your Own Review	37
8	Author's Toolbox	42
9	Odds & Ends	66
10	Writing References	77
	Study Guide Worksheet	82

About the Author

Connect with the Author Online

More Books by Author

Books Coming Soon

FORWARD

Have you ever wondered how to get noticed by a book reviewer? Keep reading. I have written this guide for you, the author, from the perspective of a reviewer, who is also a writer and independently published author.

As a writer, I have taken the route of self-publishing at this time, but may consider an independent publishing house or a digital publishing house for a future work. There is also a chance I may decide to go through the traditional print publishing. I still have time to decide each project on a case-by-case basis.

As a reviewer, I have seen some mistakes made by self-pubbed authors, and on rare occasion by those who went with an independent publishing house. This is where my reviewer's guide for authors comes in. I hope you will use it to improve not only the chance that a reviewer will pick up your book and give you a good review, but also, use it to improve your writing. I believe that it can help you.

What Reviewers Want:Get Inside One Reviewer's Mind is a guide that will help authors to understand more about how to get their book noticed by reviewers. They may be professional reviewers who work for literary magazines, for instance, Atlantic Monthly Books & Critics or New York Review of Books, or maybe the online Publishers Weekly. It could be a reviewer who simply loves to read and write and never considered doing book reviews until asked by author friends to do so. Whichever kind of reviewer you choose, this guide could become one of your best friends or partners in writing.

This book is aimed at the independent author who wishes to publish, but may be useful to any author. Read what pertains to you, skim what doesn't and share with others how they too can use this guide in their

Writer's Toolbox. Make sure to check out the Author's Toolbox chapter at the end of the guide. Also, check out the newly added chapter, Odd & Ends in the Print Edition. Also new in the Print Editon is the Writer's Book Reference section also, with books that are in print that can and should become a part of your "Author's Toolbox." I own a few of them, and the rest are on my to-buy-list.

1 BOOK COVERS

Always. Use. A. Cover.

No if, and, or buts about it. Use a cover. Whether you want to write for the major New York houses, an E- house, independent house, or self-publish, you need a cover.

This is, in my opinion, one of the things that is non-negotiable whether I am a writer, a reader or a reviewer. Yes, when I first started to do reviews, I did accept self-pubbed books with no covers. I found that each time, they were poorly written, atrocious grammar, and an apparent lack of edits, plus more. There were no "diamonds in the rough"to speak of. I no longer accept for review purposes, an e-book which is self-published without a cover.

It is possible to get a cover done for a decent price if you look around. If you go to the on-line community of Deviant Art and look around for people who have done commissioned work of book covers, you can see work that is top-notch quality. Often times these artists do commissioned book covers for a very reasonable price and proper credit.

You could also make your own cover, if you have the graphic skills necessary. Of course, you would need the right program, such as Adobe Photoshop, Corel's Paint Shop Pro or you could work with the free, open-source program known as GIMP. I have seen some wonderful covers that were made using this free program so it can definitely be done.

I am writing a non-fiction book that needs a cover, for example. With GIMP, a set of brushes, some time and patience, I was able to design a very nice and simple cover that conveys what my book is about. It is high quality, meets the industry standards, and looks like a book cover. It has a professional look about it, which is important in attempting to win readers over to your book. Like it or not, we do in fact, judge a book by it's cover. In the age of computers and being able to buy online, perhaps more than we have before.

Here is an important tip to remember when making your own cover. It must look and be of high quality. That means, it must be at least 300 dpi (dots per inch) which is more correctly known as ppi (pixels per inch). It cost me nothing but the time and energy involved. I must admit I have some background in graphics which is why it was perhaps easier for myself then it may be for someone with no experience in digital graphics at all. In order to fail, or succeed, you must attempt it first.

You don't need to pay hundreds or thousands of dollars to get a high quality cover for your self-pubbed book. It will cost you time and energy to research the book cover designers. You can search for Premade Book Covers in your genre of writing. For instance, Dara England of http://www.mycoverart.wordpress.com has designs that are $30.00. She does custom cover art that starts at $50.00. Each cover is exclusive which is the same for the custom art designs. No two are alike. Also, check her clearance page for more, at a much lower price. You may find something you like.

This is an option you may consider worthwhile but you must look for QUALITY work; premade does not have to equal shoddy. A good cover artist will use the fonts asked for, put the title and name you want on an already designed book cover and will remove that cover from service. That way, you don't have to worry that you'll see the same "book template cover" like so many books found on Kindle.

You will need a design that helps to convey what your book is about. If your book is a Victorian romance, you don't want a mystery cover. You want the cover to be appropriate for the genre in which you write and publish. If you are uncertain what genre you belong in, research and find the one that fits the closest to how you see your book. After that, find out what type of covers the print and digital houses use for different genres and start designing with that in mind. Do not copy someone else's design. That is stealing and it is wrong, both in the eyes of the artist, readers, and reviewers, but also the law.

You will need to check the stock photo sites for pictures that you can use for your cover. There are several things you must do, however. You must be certain that the copyright by the photographer allows for the use in commercial endeavors, that it is 300 dpi, and that there are no other rules at the stock site that need to be followed before using.

The essential point to remember from this chapter is that you want and need a quality book cover. You cannot skimp on this. If you do, be assured that both readers and reviewers will look the other way and find another book.

2 EDITING

This is the second point which is non-negotiable in my opinion. You must have your book edited. You cannot edit yourself and think that you have done a good job. I belong to several writers forums where editors are a part of the membership. Many of them are also writers, who have made it clear that they will not do the final edits themselves. They do their revisions and first edits of course, but they source out the rest of the work to other professionals in the field. Why do you think you can do your own edits when these people who are editors will not?

An editor is necessary. They know the rules of grammar and punctuation far better than you or I. They are aware of what the industry standards are for both traditional and digital print and publication. When things change, which they sometimes do, they are the ones aware of it. A good editor will help make your book the best it can be. They will ensure that your page formats are correct, line spacing, page breaks and much more are done properly. A good editor checks grammar and make sure words are spelled the right way. They can see where perhaps you have used the same word seven times in the same paragraph and help you to substitute a new word with the same or similar meaning.

You do not want to edit your own book, mainly because it is difficult to be objective about your own writing and manuscripts. On the other hand, you don't need to spend $5,000-10,000 dollars either. You want to look for someone who can give you a decent quote. Many freelance editors will give you a flat rate editing price. More commonly, they will offer a per-word quote based on sample pages which indicate what their editing and communication style is. This allows you to see the ability they have to catch your spelling, punctuation and grammar mistakes. It also allows you to see how they make changes and comments for you to use.

Now you want to know, "How do I find a good editor without breaking my bank account?" I'll try to help you, but you must remember that the old adage is true; You get what you pay for. If you pay very little for an editor, you can expect to get little in return for it. This doesn't include when some authors and freelance editors barter services, which is done on occasion.Once again, Google or any search engine will be your best friend. You need to input into the search box the following term to find out what is available.

How much does a free-lance editor cost? You'll then find some very good links that will help you to begin to research how much you should pay for a freelance editor. Remember to find out how they want the manuscript sent to them, and how long it will take. Some editors will only accept 'hard copy' or what we often call, 'snail mail', while others accept only email copies of manuscripts. Then there are those who do a mixture of the two. Find out which your possible editor prefers before you send your manuscript off to them.

Editing houses are an option you can consider, but I know little to nothing about them. Each writing board I have been a member of, or lurked at, says to stay far away from these places as possible. For that reason, I've done no research into it. I'm letting you know it is an option, but it almost assuredly will be a costly route to take. It is an expensive one for a new or self-publishing author to consider.

There are several different types of editing options available. I'll attempt to address the four that I am most aware of.

Developmental Edits: This is when an editor is involved from the conception of a manuscript through the draft process. They will make suggestions about content, organization and presentation which is based on analysis of competing works, comments of expert reviewer's, the client's market analysis, and other appropriate references. Writing, rewriting and research may be provided and sometimes the editor will suggest topics or provide information about topics for consideration of the author and client.

Substantive Edits: This is when an editor helps you to improve your manuscript by identifying and solving problems of overall clarity or accuracy. They may improve the order in which the text is presented by reorganizing sentence, paragraph or chapters. They help with improving readability and the flow of information, which can include revising text to help improve the presentation of your material. They may or may not do any or all of these things when they are doing this type of editing for you. Much will depend upon your manuscript and its needs.

Copy Edits: This is when the editor corrects spelling, grammar, syntax, punctuation, and word usage while preserving the meaning and voice of the original text. They check for consistent style and format often preparing a style sheet that documents style and format. They proofread for overall clarity and consult your preceding stage of text to compare with the latest stage in order to identify discrepancies, typographical errors and formatting problems.

Line Edits: This is also known by some as 'stylistic editor' A line editor's work may overlap with that of the substantive or copy editor. Line edits takes place after the substantive edits. A line editor normally has a large vocabulary and knows how to use it to help give your work that 'punch' it needs to take it from good to great. They make sure your voice and style are consistent throughout the manuscript and that transitions are effective, while they make sure that the book reads smoothly.

This is a very basic description of the four types of editing shown here, but it will give the self-publishing author a start at what to look for in an editor and how to know which type they are most in need of.

I included the section on types of editing in order to help you decide what you need in an editor for your book. It is because I, along with most reviewers, will not consider a book or manuscript that has not been edited for review. If we know it is an ARC or Advanced Readers Copy, which are put out by some of the publishing houses,we may consider it, but as a whole, reviewers rarely review books which are not edited. ARC books have been edited, and reviewers are aware there is often more editing to be done before the final issue of the book. Remember, all reviewers have their own policy. My policy is that it must be a finished manuscript preferably in PDF or Kindle format for reading. It must be edited. Publishers may send me an ARC for review purposes and they must let me know when the book is to be released so that I can do the review in ample time. I have evolved over the last few months since I have learned more about how to review, write, edit and publish. My rules change in accordance with that.

"Line editing and content editing are both usually done by the same editor, your main editor, whether in traditional or digital publishing, though there are many editors who see line editing as something they don't have time for, which is why they look for an author whose work is closer to "production ready" Copy editing is done by a separate editor. Occasionally a copy editor will do some minor line editing, especially if they see something egregious, but a lot of authors tend to get touchy about a copy editor who does this, because they see it as stepping into the editor/author relationship. I'm going to guess that most self-published authors are only going to want to pay for one editor, but it's a rare editor who's able to do both the editing and copy editing, and do it well on the same book. I wouldn't want to be responsible for both phases of the production cycle, because I rely on the copy editor coming along behind me to catch the many things I've missed while I've been focusing on the bigger picture."

- Angela James, Executive Editor at Carina Press

I took Angela James workshop on self-editing, ***Before You Hit Send,*** and must say that I learned so much. I would highly recommend this course to all authors, especially the ones who want to self-publish...but you must remember, this is only for you to self-edit before it is sent off to someone else to do in depth edits. This doesn't take the place of an editor. It is a supplement.

The essential point to remember from this chapter is that you need an editor. You need to research their methods and cost. You do not want to scrimp on this step, but neither do you want to betaken to the cleaners. You can use, for example the autocrit above to give you a quick guide to what is wrong and try to work on it yourself before you hire an editor. Above all, do your edits, then find an editor to do more edits. Readers and reviewers both will thank you.

3 CRITIQUES & BETA READERS

Many authors who are self-publishing have not considered critique groups or beta readers. These are people who will critique your manuscript in an honest manner. It's one of the easier steps in my opinion to achieve and it is one which is available for free. There are numerous sites for writers on the Internet. You need to find the one that best suites your needs. Most often, this will be the genre you write in. Once you are established there, have read their rules about how critiques are done and what is expected from all participants, you can get someone to do a thorough read of your manuscript and tell you their honest opinion of what they think of it. They can tell you if it feels too slow in places, or doesn't make sense and much more.

A Beta reader is defined by Wikipedia as follows: *"Someone who reads a written work with a critical eye, and with the aim to improve grammar, spelling, characterization and the general style of the story before it is released to the general public."*

Again, a Beta reader should not cost you to find. This is another time when a writing forum will be an invaluable tool for you when you are a writer who is looking to publish.

Why is this important to me when I am a reviewer? Why is it included here is what you really want to know. It is because when you have someone who can critique your work in an honest manner outside of an editor, or have a beta reader who can help to find those last little things, it will help to make or break your book, so why give it up without a try. When an author informs me that their book has been through a critique group and/or a beta reader or two, I know that they are taking their writing seriously. This means that the book is much more apt to be well-done. That makes reviews much easier to do.

Your essential lesson from this chapter is that a critique group or a beta reader is a tool to use in your writer's arsenal. It can be one of the most helpful tools you will use with each book. Most critiques and beta readers are also writers or editors. This can prove to be a good thing for your manuscript. Don't pass this up, please.

4 CHARACTERIZATION, PLOTS & MORE

This is where many reviewers may differ on what they are looking for when they read. Some only read books that are in first person, or third but not second, for example. I have no problem with what point of view a book is written in so long as it is consistent through the book. For most authors, they stay in one point of view throughout a book. This makes it easier on the reader, so they don't get confused by whose point of view it is.

Those who are putting out a book, should already be well aware of what point of view or P.O.V. is. If not, stop writing and Google it to find out and learn. This is essential.

Characterization is another essential element to writing and it must be consistent. This is one of the main things that most reviewers are looking for. An example is, if Jane begins the book and is a shy, retiring female, and at the end of the book, she is a go-getter, but you have shown us no transformation and no explanation has been given, then Jane is not being characterized consistently.

Are your main characters fleshed out enough? Do we know enough about them to make sense to the whole story, or are there things missing about them that would have helped us to know why Jane suddenly turned into a fearless adventurer?

As a reviewer, I look at how a character makes me feel. When I am reading about Jane, being a shy woman, does it make me feel that is within her character, or does it feel forced? I am also looking at dialog between characters. Is it believable, for the character, the story or the time period it is set in? Is it consistent and within the right parameters?

Reviewers are also looking at the plot line. Yes, I'm saying that word again. Is it consistent? Is Jane's dress light blue on page four and then dark purple on page five with no evidence of a dress change? Do the time line and the events make sense in the order they are presented? Does the plot flow well and make sense or is it plodding along and confusing? We are also looking at the plot to see if it was effective or coherent.

Most reviewers are looking at the point of view, characters and plot We look at not only the main plot, but sub-plots as well. This also applies to characters. Do these all mesh well together or do they feel piecemeal? You need to make sure your character Jane belongs on a bungee cord in the second chapter, when you told us in the first chapter how frightened of heights she is. If we learn through the book while it progresses, that she's been working on this fear and is now out on the bungee cord, it will make more sense to the reader.

The pace of a story is something that I usually feel. Sometimes, a story plods along and feels off, while another story may move slow and be right. This also works in reverse with moving too fast and having the feeling I'm in a whirlwind for no good reason, while a different author's work moves at a brisk pace and feels right. I look at pacing myself in conjunction with the storyline and often the characters. For instance, I am reviewing a book right now that moves at a fast clip. It makes total sense within the storyline, plot and for the characters.

Another story I read had the pacing off considerably. It slugged along here, dashed too fast there and didn't make sense overall. You need to be aware of the pacing issues, and this is where a beta reader or critique group is helpful. They can help you to see where you move too fast or slow. Your editor will often pick up the issues regarding the pace of the story also, but try to find it first yourself. In my opinion, the earlier you find the issue, the easier it will be to fix.

If you take only one essential lesson away from this chapter, I hope it is to realize that your plot, storyline, characters and the pace of the story really go together. If a slow moving Jane is dumped into a fast-paced story, it doesn't feel right, and the story feels off all the way around. Make sure your character belongs in THAT storyline, with that plot.

5 FINDING A REVIEWER FOR YOUR BOOK

Some may think this is easy. It is not. Though many new authors will sit down and write every reviewer on a list they find, this is a bad way to get a review. Why? Because you haven't found out if the book you want them to read is even in a genre they review. You need to sit down and use a search engine. Do a search for book reviewers first. What I found was Book Review Services. Most of these places charge a fee for reviewing an authors book. I personally would not be willing to pay a book review service, but that's up to you.

I then input "Author looking for Book Reviewer" and got some better hits for pages. One of the first ones to come up was ***smartbitchestrashybooks.com*** which reviews Romance genre books. They would not be the ones to send your Paranormal Thriller to. You're getting a bit closer, but you have to do a lot of work to find out who on this list of websites you Googled will review your Paranormal Thriller. So, let's try this.

Input the genre you wrote your book in. For instance, for your Paranormal Thriller book, I'd input "Paranormal Thriller Book Reviewers." You now have a more precise list of reviewers and you're more apt to find someone who reviews this genre. I'll allow you to go through the list to find ones that match what you are looking for in a reviewer.

Let's assume now, that you have found reviewers for your genre. What's next? Well, now you go through each reviewers site to find out what their review policies are. How do they want a book submitted, do they review self-pubbed or only authors with a traditional or e-pub house? Are you sure they review the genre you wrote your book in, double check here. Do they have a length of book they prefer to read or not read? Follow these guidelines exactly to have the best chance for a reviewer to want to read your book. If they say to send a query letter to them with some information regarding the book, do so, following their instructions closely.

Don't send them the whole book yet. It's likely to get 'trashed' and no response back, since you didn't take the time to follow the guidelines that were in place. When they ask for the book, send it in the manner they request. Most will request an "attachment" of a PDF or if you are on Smashwords and have a coupon code they can use for a free copy, that is acceptable to most, because they can download the book in the format that suites them best. For me, I accept PDF, Kindle and E-Pub. I can read these on my Windows machine. Other reviewers will ask for other formats according to their needs.

As you can see, how they request a book will vary greatly. What books they review is also entirely up to the reviewers choice. Don't try to get a Romance reviewer to review your Horror book. You won't enjoy the results if they do. Find a reviewer who is actually interested in the genre. There are more than enough book reviewers out there to find one that suites your purposes.

Most reviewers have a contact page, that states exactly how to contact them. Often, they also have a Review Guideline that states what they review, how they review it, how long a review will take and how to request a review. Use this. Always. This is your best bet to get a reviewer interested in your book. It shows that you took the time to read their guidelines and how they do things, rather than assuming all reviewer's are the same. We are not.

Contact them according to the instruction's given. They are there for a reason and following them will tend to endear you to the reviewer, though they still may not enjoy your book. Yes, this does happen. It's truly not personal. Remember, a book reviewers review is subjective. It's an opinion, but doesn't necessarily reflect personally on you. I've read some books by people I consider friends, and given their books a review of only being mediocre. It wasn't personal, and they understood that. I told them what I liked and what I didn't. Other books by the same people I gave rave reviewers because they were that good.

If, by chance, the reviewer doesn't have any guidelines posted but does have a contact email, then I would say it would be alright to send one email to them with the following question and information provided. For subject line, write something similar to this: Query: What are your review guidelines?

Include the rest of this within the body of the email you are sending. Remember, do not add attachments to this query letter.

- Your Name *(You can use the pen name you wrote the book under if you prefer.*

- Title of Book

- Genre of Book

- Length of Book

- *Publishers*

- Date Published or Date To Be Released

- Format available *(Kindle, PDF, Print, E-pub, etc.)*

- Your email address for them to contact you back. *(Put their contact email in your contact list so it won't mark anything they send back to be spam.)*

After you've given this information, you can then ask in the body of the email whether they are still doing reviews, and if so, what their guidelines are. Again, do

NOT send an attachment at this time. They'll ask you for it if they want it. By having this information already available, it gives them something to think about and they may or may not say yes. If they do not respond within two weeks, I would say you could send a short follow-up email, reminding them about your previous request. After that, do nothing. They obviously aren't interested.

Use your time to find a new reviewer. You may get numerous, No answers from people, or sometimes you may get, not right now, but check back later. File those Check Back later ones, and DO SO! Keep an eye on their reviewers blog and see when they are accepting submissions for reviews again, in your genre or at all. I try to keep my guidelines updated to let you know when I am accepting, and if I am not, I tell a short reason why and how long I expect to not be able to do so. This is why you must be faithful in checking back at the reviewer's guideline page about reviews so that you do not have to keep sending an email to see if they are reviewing yet. If after 3 months, there is still no work on their reviewing status, I'd say to move on to another reviewer.

What essential points should you take from this chapter? I think two things. The first being you need to know what a reviewer wants to read, and if your book fits that, then follow the guidelines that are set out by that particular reviewer. Follow them, and a reviewer is more apt to say yes. It's going to take work to find a reviewer. Persevere. There is one out there that will be willing to read your book.

The second thing would be that you don't take a reviewer's opinion of your book personal. It's not directed at you that they don't care for the book, it is something about the book that didn't sit well with them. Pacing, plot, or something else was off in their opinion.

6 THE REVIEWER'S REVIEW: HOW TO RESPOND

This one can get sticky. Do you respond to a reviewer's review, or do you let it go? What if it's a fantastic review about your book? Or, maybe it totally skewered your book. What do you do?

From a reviewer's point of view, I say you do nothing. Seriously. Most especially, do not respond to a negative review by spouting off on how the reviewer is clueless or what not. It is not they who will look bad, but you, the author. A reviewer has their own opinion.

He didn't find your book to his/her satisfaction If they have said in the review, what made them mark it down, read that carefully. Are they talking about the plot being unrealistic, the characters boring, the editing abysmal or non-existence. Are they talking about typographical errors that should have been caught already? Find out by reading the and then stepping away from it and not responding.

If you feel you must respond, I would say respond in a respectful email to them and ask exactly what they found wrong, besides what they may have already said and if you might send them an edited copy if the mistake was you sent an unedited copy. We reviewers understand that this can and does happen. Accept that if this is the case, it was your mistake and the review was based on what you did send them. They may or may not be willing to amend a review if you approach them in a calm and respectful manner.

So, the reviewer totally raved about your book and you're dancing with glee. You want to shout to the world about how wonderful this reviewer is. Don't. Many authors will send a private email to the reviewer thanking them for a positive review. This is acceptable. Please don't post in public on the reviewer's blog, for often this keeps readers from responding to the review who might otherwise. By maintaining a lurking position on the reviewers blog, you can see how readers are affected by your work. Sometimes, you must take it with a grain of salt, but isn't that just life? Now, if you're in a private writing group or forum and want to say how stoked you are by a great review, go for it, and please, place a link to the review. Maybe others will want to read it as well. It might even generate new books for the reviewer to critique and rate

Some authors that I know respond with a short, polite private email to all reviewer's regardless of how the review went. I think this is a good policy, because it gets the word through the reviewing community that

"X author" is a total pro to work with, and is always nice and respectful no matter what the review. This counts in the book reviewers' world and in the authors world. When an author gets a 'biotch author" title, no one wants to work with them. Your fame truly does proceed you. Make it count. Make your claim to fame that you are easy to work with, respectful and courteous at all times.

Essential lesson to take from this chapter? Use your head when responding to any review. Think twice before commenting on the reviewer's blog directly. What you say there, will travel the internet at break-neck speeds. Ask Jacqueline Howett, or better yet, don't. She responded in a rabid way to a reviewer and other commentors regarding her book. One of the people she told to f*** off was a Head Editor of a major E-Publisher. Guess who's not likely to ever publish with that company? All because she chose to respond in public to a negative review with venom and spittle. To put it in simple terms, don't do it! Not if you want a career as an author.

7 DOING YOUR OWN REVIEW

DO. NOT. DO. THIS! I don't care if the man who has a book about how to "whore yourself and your book" says it's okay. He is WRONG. 100% wrong! This is not only my opinion but the opinion of numerous authors, reviewers, publicists, agents and readers. It is dishonest. It is unethical. Don't get caught in this trap.

By the same token, do not ask your family and best friends to review the book either. They are not objective. Find someone independent and unbiased. It may take time and work, but in the end, you'll know the reviews are honest and above board.

I know of two authors to date that I have proof have not only reviewed their own books, but they have had friends and family do it. In one of the cases, they used a dead man's name to review a book. A man I knew well who would have been appalled to have his name linked with that book.

Readers figured out quickly due to the exact same phrasing, words, sentence structures of the different reviews that one person was doing them...most likely the author. It fit the way the book was written. This only makes you, the author, look bad and dishonest. Is this the legacy you want for your books? I know I don't.

Readers don't trust authors who review their own books, or get family to do it. Now, I must say, I did review one of my husband's books, but when I first started reading it, we were barely dating. I stated clearly that I was the authors wife and that I started reading it before our marriage. I was up front about it. That is one reason I am not ashamed of having done it.

Given the same circumstances, however, I would not review his books. I'm no longer objective where his writing is concerned. I believe this is the difference between having family or friends review it, but not acknowledging who they are, and having those same people review your book and stating exactly who they are. I've seen far too many of these in the past year or so, that don't acknowledge their relationship to the author. It's still not a wise idea though. It's the reason I no longer will do it. I did it once and being a reviewer now, I see how it doesn't look right. I don't mind learning from my mistakes. I hope you can as well.

Is there an essential point to this chapter? Yes. Take this chapter seriously. If you don't, you could damage your reputation beyond repair, before it even gets started.

Don't review your own book. Don't have family or close friends review your book. Find unbiased, objective people to do so. Those are the honest reviews that readers are looking for. Readers are a smart bunch. They can spot a phony faster than Superman could catch Lois Lane. Don't let them catch you trying to pull a fast one. They'll not be quiet about how they feel. The internet moves too fast to think that you won't get caught and that if you do, no one will hear about it. Just ask the authors who have done their own reviews and got caught. Their book sales are pretty much stalled now, if they have any at all.

It's not worth your reputation as an author to mess with this. Keep your reputation unsullied. It's what is going to help you to sell your books. That plus excellent, well-edited manuscripts.

Now, go get writing. What are you waiting for? You can't publish it, if you haven't written it yet.

8 AUTHOR'S TOOLBOX

I've given you things to think about and ideas to research, so what kind of friend would I be if I didn't give an author some idea of places to go for help and learning. I've included things that are not covered in this guide in order to try to help you have as much information at hand in one place as possible. There are numerous print books out there to consider. Google about writing, editing, etc, and then start sifting through the sites.

Some things that those who are self-publishing want or need to consider are the following:

Price Points: How and Why to Set them

As a new author, who is self publishing, you may want to concentrate more on getting copies sold, which gets your name out there among the readers, reviewers and other authors, and worry about making a decent income at a later date. Unless you get SUPER lucky, you won't be having "The Next Great Novel" up on Amazon, B&N or other places. Think about it, Amanda Hocking self pubbed for quite a long time, before she got noticed. She want for more readers rather than price. Now, she can set higher prices when self publishing a book and sell fairly well.

Does this mean you have to sell at $0.99? Nope. You need to figure out, for you, what the lowest price you can afford, based on several factors.

Length of Book

Most eBooks under 10-15K words tend to well at $0.99. Books over 80K can be priced higher...probably closer to $5.99-9.99. The higher the word count, the higher the price can be, but rarely will anyone pay more than $9.99 for an eBook. It may take time to find the right price, but with Amazon, Barnes and Noble and Smashwords, changing the price is very simple and usally less than 72 hours. Smashwords is pretty much instant, but Amazon and Barnes and Noble are still the bigger book sellers and where most people still get their books from.

Print books are different. It costs more to actually produce them, and distribution. That's why often paperbacks start at around $9.99 on up. Self publishing yourself through Lightening Source, or Create Space, the two I know are legitimate and work well with Amazon and other distribution centers allow you to set your own price. With CreateSpace, there is a minimum it can sell for, but you want to remember to make at least a little profit. Don't get greedy though. It costs to make changes to the book once it's published. Set a reasonable price that meets the minimum required and gives you a small royalty. You'll need to find the "sweet spot" for you book, your genre.

Genre

Fiction sells better than non- fiction. Non-Fiction tends to not do as well at lower prices, so $2.99 tends to be a decent "low" price for the non-fiction eBook. This isn't always true. My eBook of "What Reviewers Want: Get Inside One Reviewer's Mind" is doing decent at $0.99 cents. It got its momentum during a 3 day free spurt via Amazon Kindle Select. *(More on this later)*

You'll need to do some research to find out what the going price on your genre tends to be. You don't want to overprice your book and keep readers away, nor do you want to undercut your price and have it devalued. Find the price that works best for you. Don't use the Traditional or eBook publisher prices as a guideline, as they are very often priced considerably higher to adjust for costs of publishing, etc.

Again, print is different. It still sells better at a slightly higher price than fiction, but not always. Again, genre can affect the cost of a print book. Many people seem willing to pay a bit more for say, a Mystery than they will for romance. Take these things into consideration when pricing your book.

Debut Author or Established Author

An established author, such as Gemma Halliday, Nora Roberts, Stephen King will be more likely to get away with setting higher prices on their self-published works than the debut author. (Not that I know if Nora Roberts actually self-publishers. I do know that Stephen King did, and Gemma Halliday does.)

One of the reasons why is because they bring with them readers from their already published works from publishing houses. This is important. Their names are already known, at least to some degree.

A debut author brings no readers in. It's their first book and no one is quite certain if they're up to the challenge of writing a book and making it work. It might not sound fair, but this is how it is. It makes sense. I have little readership as I only have a few books out. I recognize I have to work hard, promote more and market better to compete in the book market. I think there's plenty of room for more books and authors, but we need to keep the quality of the work as high as possible.

Stand Alone Title or Series

Stand alone titles will most often sell for less than books that are in a series. When an author is writing a series, her readers know there are more books to come, especially if the first book indicates it is part of a trilogy, such as Crista McHugh's with **The Soulbearer Trilogy.** I can't really say just why it is, but I know even for myself that it's true.

With a series, many of the self-published authors will put the first book in a series that is published in eBook format at 99¢ to get the interest of readers for the rest of the series. They then often will raise the price of the first book after a set amount of time back to its original price. So far, this seems to have worked well for a number of the authors I stay in contact with. It is something for you to consider when pricing. It draws readers in, who may otherwise not read your work, and if the quality is above par, keeps them around, ready to buy your next book in the series.

Important: Be flexible with your price. My husband put out a good book with nearly 64K words. It sat with no sales for 4 months. Not one. We lowered the price to $3.99. One sale in one month now. No promotion. I can't see taking it lower than that at this point, so we're going to ratchet up the promotions and marketing

There really isn't a set price that you can just arbitrarily look at and price a book. You need to do research to figure out where to start pricing your book and how high is too high. This brings me to my next point for indie authors to think about.

How to promote and/or market? Why?

The best way to promote your book is to start **BEFORE** you finish the book. Blog about it. Get others to blog. Get reviews before it comes out. Get it on Facebook. Tweet it on Twitter. Bring attention to your book.

But, D. L. WHY? Because, it helps you to get your name out in front of readers. Getting Advanced reading copies to reviewers allows them time to review it, and if there are some mistakes not caught in editing, many will tell you about it and agree to hold off on the review until a later date, with a revised copy. As a reviewer, we understand the Advanced Readers Copy may change before final publishing, so we're willing to help the author make it better.

How to do this?

Twitter

Start a personal account and begin by just getting to know Twitter.Customize your personal profile. Remember to do your bio. Add your website URL. If you choose, you can connect to Facebook from here. That's a personal choice. I do, but many do not.

Learn how to do re-tweets, replies. Get acquainted with other "Tweeples" (Twitter people). Learn the lay of the land before you ever begin to promote your upcoming book. Go ahead and mention you're a writer. If someone asks about the book, make it short and sweet. (140 characters or less). As time gets closer to when you want to release, say 2 months or so, begin to slowly start talking more directly about the book. No more than one tweet an hour of promotion.

Make sure you are also tweeting other information that has nothing to do with your book. Otherwise, you may be marked spam by users or by Twitter. Personally, I try to do this once every 2-3 days only. If someone asks more, of course answer. It's good publicity. Just don't over do it. It's not necessary. You want to learn how to interact with other people on twitter. Chatting of a sort.

Learn how to make lists in Twitter. It will speed things up when going through tweets. Follow other authors, editors, publishers. Learn what they are doing, how they do it. Interact, but DO NOT try to sell your book to any editor or publisher. Seriously. It's the fastest way to being blocked and trust me, editors and publishers will let one another know which authors do this. So, please, don't be one of those who does.

Also, learn how to use hashtags (#). This can be very helpful to get your tweets going toward the people you want them to go to. For instance, if you are looking for a cover designer and want to tweet that, use #BookCover or #BookCoverDesign within your trweet.

You might get someone to answer. You just never know whose out there in Twitterland.

Facebook Pages

Set up a Facebook Page at Facebook. You will need a Facebook Profile first. (Personal Page) When you go to create it, choose Artist/Band/Public Figure. There is an option there for "Author". That's what you want.

Set it up, and don't forget to try to class it up a bit. Now that Pages have the Timeline (as of March 31, 2012), you can create a Timeline cover that tells more about you, your books. Just remember to read the Facebook Terms of Use. No URL's are allowed on the cover. Your book covers are allowed. Create a landing page. You can use Static HTML app, iand add it to your page. Then go back to your page and begin to set up the page. There are a number of ways to customize it, including having "Fans Only" content. You get to decide. You can add images also. Just make sure you have permission to use them.

Google+

Set up a Google+ account through your Google Account, if you have Gmail. Post your book covers in the photo area. Like Twitter, get a feel for Google+ before jumping in and trying to sell your as yet unpublished book. By the way, you can link Twitter to your Google+ account. Do a search to see just how. It's easy. Now, let's move on, shall we?

Pen Names

Figure out what name you want to write under. Your real name, a pen name. Several pen names across different genres. Then, do an internet search for that name/pen name. See what kind of publicity it already has. I researched two names I wanted to use, before settling on the one I have for my Erotic Romance writing. Why did I not go with my original pen names? Because someone within the publish field already had the name and it had a bad reputation.

Try to avoid using the same name as another writer where possible. It causes problems. My husband, Rob Graham knows this, as there is another author Rob Graham, whose work shows up listed with his, and we have to send emails to get it removed from my husband's profiles at Amazon, Goodreads, etc. It's a pain, and if possible, can often be avoided. Add an initial if need be, if your name is the same as another.

For instance, let's assume your name is Nora Roberts. For real. Your middle name is Clarissa. So, perhaps you can go by the name of N. Clarissa Roberts, or Nora C. Roberts. Something that distinguishes you from this well-known author, or in my husband's case, not so well-known. Save all of you a headache and make it easier for readers to find you. However, if you write the same genre as a well-known author, your best bet is the first example. N. Clarissa Roberts. Or, perhaps, but I don't know, Nora Clarissa Roberts could also work. Just try to avoid intentionally cashing in on another authors name.

The reason I wanted to discuss the pen name/real name issue, is because when you get ready to set up your website and/or blog, you're going to need to know what name you're going to use. Whenever possible, try to get the URL/Domain name with the name you want to write under. Remember, there are people out there who "park" domains to try to cash in on wanting that name. Using the example above, if you need to, you can always attempt to go for the n.clarissaroberts.com domain. This makes it easy to find you.

Website/Blog

I'm going to assume you've already have your domain name and you're ready to start on your website. I assume this, because I hope you'll have done it before getting to this stage. Finish your website or blog before you open your doors to the public. People hate to see "Under Construction" signs on websites. If you can afford a web designer, go ahead, you'll most likely have this site a long time, so make the investment now. It will pay off in the end. You can always Google for some of the free website builders out there, such as the newer Wix and others, but remember, they tend to come and go. I had a Geocities for nearly 13 years, and then, poof, gone.

Many people set up on a paid WordPress site which allows for incorporating a blog, or as I do, use the free WordPress site. There are a number of good ones out there. Do your research and find the one that meets your needs. For me, simple and blog format meets my needs. For others, a full website is what they wanted and needed.

If you know how to do graphics, you can design your own theme. Using WordPress or Blogger, you can find free or paid themes and customize them. Use banners. Go easy on too many garish colors. Consider your readers. Red text on black background, I'm gone. I can't read it, and I don't care. Yes, I've left major author pages for this problem.

Writing Back Cover or E-Book Blurbs

Writing a blurb is not really easy but neither is it that hard. You want to capture your readers attention as quickly as possible. You don't want to give the story away, but you do want to convey to some degree what it's about and get the readers attention so they'll buy the book. You have about 150-200 words in which to do this, as many readers never move past the blurb or short description on Amazon, or other book seller sites. With your ebook, you want to really try to get the reader's attention as quickly as possible and keep their attention. There are so many books out there you are competing against. Though, in my opinion, it's not really a competition at all. I think there is more than enough room for all of the authors, but we need to ramp up the quality of independent published books.

This is true about print also. Many people turn over the book to read the back blurb. That's how much time you have to capture their attention. Use it wisely.

Learn how to write blurbs that give the most information without giving away the story. Normally, not more than two, for shorter books or three to four paragraphs at the most for longer books. One way to learn is to pull down the books you own already. Look at the book's back cover. See how their blurbs are written. How many paragraphs, how characters are introduced, or plot and story. The language and voice of the blurb often helps to set the tone of the book. Use this to your advantage.

Writing Front Cover Blurbs

Here you have even less time to get their attention. You have at the most about 2 lines, maybe 7-10 words. Use action verbs to convey as much as possible in as short of words necessary. "Fast-Paced! Exciting. A Real Adventure!" This gets their attention. Of course if it's a romance, you'll want to use more romantic, sensual words. "An epic love story." You get the idea. Learn to write these short and sweet.

Kindle Select Program

The Kindle Select Program is by Amazon. It allows authors to make their book exclusive to Amazon for 90 days. During that time, you have five (5) days you can make your book free. This can be a boon to new authors, such as myself, as it gets people to look at your book. In fact, with the eBook version of **What Reviewers Want: Get Inside One Reviewer's Mind**, I had 200 copies downloaded over three days, and then received two 5-star reviews!

This was a good thing. It also got me on the *Also Bought* list, which is important, as it gets you book out in front of more people. This eBook version now shows up regularly with other writing books. This puts it in front of our readers once again. You want this.

For those who are more established and have had good sales without Kindle Select, I've heard from a number of authors that it isn't such a good idea then.

Many of them actually **LOST** money using Kindle Select.

A new author can get noticed and perhaps begin to make some money. Remember, your mileage may vary though. For me, getting the reviews made the free days worth while for me. Figure out why you expect from Kindle Selects Program, and its free days, and what is most important to you. For me, reviews and more exposure to my readers was more important than making a little money. I know that will come along as people begin to read my works and I prove myself a worthwhile author.

In the end, this must be your decision. You'll want to talk to established authors, go to writing forums, and of course, do your own research so you can figure out if this is what you want or need.

9 ODDS & ENDS

Self-Publishing Checklist

For Print

- Finish your manuscript.

- Edit your manuscript.

- Format for eBook or for Print. There is a difference.

- Begin blogging or start your author website while writing your book.

- Get a book cover designed, or do it yourself, but please, make it
look professional as possible.

- Consider if you need an ISBN. Based on where you decide to sell from.

- Consider obtaining copyright. **This isn't necessary, but can be helpful if you are plagiarized and decide to pursue legal steps.**

- Consider starting your own Doing Business As (DBA) or LLC (Limited Liability Corporation). This allows you to publish under a publishing name rather than using Amazon, Smashwords, or CreateSpace as the publisher. Seek legal advice if you have any questions.

- Decide on where to get books printed/published. Consider Lightening Source or CreateSpace. There are pros and cons to each. Research to see which is best for you as a new, self-publishing author.

- Save your file in a PDF file. You'll need this.

- Create an account at wherever you have chosen to publish your book.

- Upload files to your publishing company.

- If you intend to sell on Amazon, set up an Amazon Author Account.

- **For eBook**

- Choose your publishing platform. Smashwords, Amazon, Barnes & Noble, etc. Also consider selling the PDF file from your own website/blog. Do research to decide if this will work for you.

- Format your eBook template. Upload .doc format to Smashwords and Amazon.

- Upload the .doc formatted files to your publishing platform.

Marketing/Promotion

- Sign up for the social media of your choice. Facebook, Twitter, LinkedIn, and YouTube, if you plan to use book trailers.

- Create a blog. Start blogging. Make it fun, informative. Don't be all about selling/promoting your book. You want to get readers, not alienate them.

- Begin to look for places you can guest blog at. Often, within your own genre. Find out what their rules are about promoting. FOLLOW THEM.

- Begin to look at Virtual Book Tours. Find other authors that are wanting to blog also and set up a blog tour so that you can each promote your books to new readers.

- Write a Press Release. Sometimes, you are asked what your book is about, having a press release already made up helps you to answer short and sweet without forgetting key points. You never know when you might be trapped in an elevator with an editor. Keep it with you. Consider it an important paper to never go anywhere without. You might not need it, but you just never know.

Writing a Synopsis

Have I confused you? Not my intention. I recommend learning how to write a synopsis because it can help you to learn to write your own book in a tighter, less wordy manner. It is also beneficial, should you ever decide you want to publish through an e-publisher or print publisher.

You'll want to write a 1-2 page synopsis. Read the guidelines of any publisher you think you may be interested in at some time and learn to do it to fit their format guidelines. Just remember, each publisher will be different. Some will want it single-spaced, some double-spaced.

Bascially, you want to tell the high points of your story and also include how the story resolves itself. Yes, that's right. You want to tell any editor who may read the synopsis, how the story ends.

As I've said countless times in this book, continue to do your own research to find out what publishers want, what they expect when you submit to them, etc. It's not a one-size fits all world out there when it comes to publiishing.

Query Letters

Nathan Bransford explains it best, in my opinion on what a query letter is:

"A query letter is part business letter, part creative writing exercise, part introduction, part death defying leap through a flaming hoop. (Don't worry, you won't catch fire and die during the query process though it may feel precisely like that at times). In essence: it is a letter describing your project."

He also tells us to, what's that dear authors? That's right...Research. See, I'm not the only one telling you that research is important and necessary. As you've noticed by now, it's needed for many t hings to do with self-publishing, and it's very helpful in writing a query letter. Now, why does Nathan want you to research?

- You want to figure out which agent might be a good fit for your project. Not all agents are alike, just as not all authors are alike.

- You want to figure out the agent's submission procedure.

- You'll want to include a personalized tidbit about the agent in your query, to show that you have done your research.

- Make sure there are no spelling or grammar errors in your query letter. This is often the first thing that an agent or an editor will see. Like it or not, you will almost assuredly be judged on your writing within the query letter.

There is much more to writing a query letter, but you already know what I shall say. Research it. Trust me, you'll remember it longer and better if you do the research.

I hope that this short book has been informative to you, the author who is getting ready to self-publish. It's meant to be a help, not a hindrance. I wanted to share with you the things I have learned over the past three years as I decided to seriously go into writing and publishing. I still have much to learn, but feel that when we have wisdom to share, that we should.

Please take the things written here as a guideline. Each author is different. Their needs are different. Take from this book, the things that will help. Just remember, you want to research your options for all the things I've discussed, learn how to do them to the best of you ability and to put out a quality eBook or Print book.

Please don't skimp when you don't have to. There is no race or compettion in self-publishing. Take the time you need to learn how to do it right the first time and save yourself time, energy and money. You'll be glad you did.

10 WRITING REFERENCES FOR AUTHORS

11 Secrets to Getting Published by Mary DeMuth.

A Tree Grows in Brooklyn by Betty Smith.

Copy-editing and Proofreading for Dummies by Suzanne Gilad.

Grammar Girl's 101 Misused Words You'll Never Confuse Again by Mignon Fogerty.

Grammar Girl's Quick and Dirty Tips for Better Writing (Quick & Dirty Tips) by Mignon Fogerty.

How to Write a Book Proposal by Michael Larsen

Line by Line: How to Edit Your Own Writing by Claire Kehrwald Cook.

Merriam-Webster's Guide to Punctuation and Style by Merriam-Webster.

Nail Your Novel: Why Writers Abandon Books and How You Can Draft, Fix and Finish With Confidence by Roz Morris.

On Writing by Stephen King.

Online Book Marketing: The Least Expensive, Most Effective Ways to Create Book Buzz by Lorraine Phillips.

Plot and Structure: (Techniques and Exercises for Crafting a Plot that Grips the Reader From Start to Finish.) (Write Great Fiction) by James Scott Bell.

Self-Editing for Fiction Writers: How to Edit Yourself into Print (2nd Ed.) by Renne Browne and Dave King.

The Blue Book of Grammar and Punctuation: An Easy-to-Use Guide with Clear Rules, Real-World Examples, and Reproducible Quizzes by Mignon Fogerty.

The Chicago Manual of Style (16th Ed.) by University of Chicago Press Staff.

The Complete Idiot's Guide to Getting Your Romance Published by Julie Beard.

The Copyright Handbook: How to Protect and Use Written Words (4th ed.) by Stephen Fishman.

The Elements of Style (4th Ed.) by William Strunk and E.B. White.

The Essential Guide to Getting Your Book Published: How to Write it, Sell it, and Market it...Successfully by David Henry Sterry and Arielie Eckstut.

The Self-Publishing Manual: How to Write, Print, and Sell Your Own Book, (15th Ed.) by Dan Poynter.

The Sell Your Novel Toolkit by Elizabeth Lyon.

The Wrong Word Dictionary by Dave Dowling.

Write the Perfect Book Proposal: 10 That Sold and Why (2nd Ed.) by Jeff Herman and Deborah Levine Herman.

Writing Fiction for Dummies by Randy Ingermanson and Peter Economy.

Your Novel Proposal: From Creation to Contract by Blythe Carmenson and Marshall J. Cook.

WHAT REVIEWERS WANT: GET INSIDE ONE REVIEWER'S MIND

Study Guide Worksheet For Authors

Here are some questions you may want to ask yourself now that you've read this guide. These are questions just for you. I do recommend either using a pen/paper or making a list online for yourself. Whichever you find most comfortable to do. I have given you a page for each question to write answers, but you may need more room.

If you are in an author's group using this guide, you and your group members may or may not want to discuss these questions and your answers outloud. Again, each group will differ in the way the decide how to best use this worksheet. Remember to be honest with yourself in answering these questions. It will benefit you in the end.

You have my permission to copy the pages with questions that follow for insertion into binder/folder.

For **PERSONAL USE** only. Not to be reprinted for any other reason, or used in any other material.

D. L. GRAHAM

WHAT REVIEWERS WANT: GET INSIDE ONE REVIEWER'S MIND

- **Why do you want to self-publish?**

WHAT REVIEWERS WANT: GET INSIDE ONE REVIEWER'S MIND

- What are your expectations in self-publishing?

WHAT REVIEWERS WANT: GET INSIDE ONE REVIEWER'S MIND

- **What is Characterization? Story Arc? Plot? Pacing? Voice? POV?** *You should already know this, if you're planning to publish anywhere.*

WHAT REVIEWERS WANT: GET INSIDE ONE REVIEWER'S MIND

- Why do I need someone else to edit for me? Can I do self-edits at all?

WHAT REVIEWERS WANT: GET INSIDE ONE REVIEWER'S MIND

- What is the difference between a beta reader and a critiquer? Do I need both?

WHAT REVIEWERS WANT: GET INSIDE ONE REVIEWER'S MIND

- Have I read any books on honing my writing, editing? Which ones? Were they helpful?

WHAT REVIEWERS WANT: GET INSIDE ONE REVIEWER'S MIND

- Have I read any books on marketing or promotion? Which ones? Were they helpful?

WHAT REVIEWERS WANT: GET INSIDE ONE REVIEWER'S MIND

- How much money am I willing to put into self-publishing my book?

- Am I ready to publish? Self or otherwise?

ABOUT THE AUTHOR

D. L. Graham recently self-published a lesbian erotica romance: **A Woman to Love** which is available at Amazon, Barnes & Noble, and Smashwords. It is published under the name of angel Graham. **What Reviewers Want: Get Inside One Reviewer's Mind** is her first non-fiction publication. She is currently working on a second non-fiction book, an abuse memoir, and has finished a short vignette, **My Fear of You: Living with Agoraphobia. Broken Pieces of Me**, an abuse memoir and **The Masks I Wear,** a collection of original poetry are slated for a Fall/Winter 2012 release.

She is currently living in the United States, but is working on immigrating to Canada to live with her husband, Rob Graham, also an author. They are both hoping this can happen before Christmas of 2012.

CONNECT WITH THE AUTHOR ONLINE

Amazon Author Page:
http://www.amazon.com/-/e/B0063ULKOQ

Facebook:
http://www.facebook.com/angelThoughtsbyangelGraham

Goodreads:
http://www.goodreads.com/author/show/5221979.Angel_Graham

Linked In
http://www.linkedin.com/profile/view?id=92129048&trk=tab_pro

Smashwords:
http://www.smashwords.com/profile/view/hisangel

Twitter : http://twitter.com/angel_graham

My Blog: http://angelgrahamauthor.wordpress.com/

MORE BOOKS BY D. L. GRAHAM

My Fear of You: Living with Agoraphobia is a short vignette that explores the life of the author, who struggles each day with agoraphobia, a fear of crowds, people, enclosed and also wide-open spaces. Spaces where she fears she cannot get out of quickly. It includes information on treatment options, and as always, urges you to seek your own medical consultation.

A Woman to Love is written by D. L. Graham's alter ego, angel Graham. This is a tender, yet spicy lesbian erotic novelette about a submissive and a dominent who have been hurt before and now find themselves drawn to one another and also to the BDSM lifestyle. Follow Dana and Alexandria as they take their online relationship to a new level when they meet in person.

BOOKS COMING SOON

Broken Pieces of Me is a memoir that describes the authors journey to healing and hope following a childhood of verbal, emotional and sexual abuse. It's not all doom and gloom, as the author uses a more laid back way of writing her story, similar to the way she speaks. A Fall/Winter 2012 release date is hoped for.

The Masks I Wear is a collection of original poetry by D. L. Graham, many of which were written during her tumultuous teen years growing up in an abusive home. Some of the poems are "darker" in tone and may not be suitable for younger children or very sensitive individuals. A Fall/Winter 2012 rlease date is hoped for.

www.ingramcontent.com/pod-product-compliance
Lightning Source LLC
Chambersburg PA
CBHW071520040426
42444CB00008B/1734